STOCK TRADING OPTIONS

All the trading strategies for beginners, including stock market investing and forex investing. Follow these tips if you want to generate a passive income.

Brad Johnson

© **Copyright 2020 - All rights reserved.**

The content contained within this book may not be reproduced, duplicated or transmitted without direct written permission from the author or the publisher.

Under no circumstances will any blame or legal responsibility be held against the publisher, or author, for any damages, reparation, or monetary loss due to the information contained within this book. Either directly or indirectly.

Legal Notice: This book is copyright protected. This book is only for personal use. You cannot amend, distribute, sell, use, quote or paraphrase any part, or the content within this book, without the consent of the author or publisher.

Disclaimer Notice: Please note the information contained within this document is for educational and entertainment purposes only. All effort has been executed to present accurate, up to date, and reliable, complete information. No warranties of any kind are declared or implied. Readers acknowledge that the author is not engaging in the rendering of legal, financial, medical or professional advice. The content within this book has been derived from various sources. Please consult a licensed professional before attempting any techniques outlined in this book.

By reading this document, the reader agrees that under no circumstances is the author responsible for any losses, direct or indirect, which are incurred as a result of the use of information contained within this document, including, but not limited to, — errors, omissions, or inaccuracies.

TABLE OF CONTENTS

INTRODUCTION 6

CHAPTER 1:   THE WORLD'S GREATEST OPPORTUNITY MACHINE 12
- WHY USE OPTIONS? 12
- HOW OPTIONS WORK 13
- CONS OF OPTIONS TRADING 13
- HOW MUCH CAPITAL IS NEEDED? 14

CHAPTER 2:   HOW TO GET STARTED WITH STOCK 16
- OPTIONS TRADING ACCOUNT 16
- STEPS TO OPEN A TRADING ACCOUNT 19
- 7 EASY STEPS TO START OPTIONS TRADING 21

CHAPTER 3:   DAY TRADING OPTIONS THAT ACTUALLY WORKS 22
- CALL OPTIONS 22
- PUT OPTIONS 23
- USING CALL AND PUT OPTIONS TO MAKE A PROFIT 23
- STYLES OF OPTIONS 24
- AMERICAN OPTIONS 25
- EUROPEAN OPTIONS 25
- EXTRAORDINARY OPTIONS 26
- BERMUDA OPTIONS 26
- BARRIER OPTIONS 26
- BASKET OPTIONS 27
- CAPPED STYLE OPTIONS 28
- COMPOUND OPTIONS 28
- LOOKBACK OPTIONS 28
- ASIAN OPTIONS 28
- BINARY OPTIONS 29
- FORWARD START OPTIONS 29
- LEAPS 29
- INDEX OPTIONS 30

CHAPTER 4:   SECRETS OF THE STOCK MARKET 32
- WHAT IS LEVERAGED INVESTING? 33
- COVERED CALL WRITING 34
- CALENDAR SPREAD TRADING 36

CHAPTER 5:   WHY STOCKS ARE GOOD INVESTMENTS 38
- LIMIT YOUR RISK 38
- BETTER LEVERAGE FOR THE MONEY 39
- HIGHER PERCENTAGE OF RETURNS 40

HELPS TO HEDGE INTRADAY OR FUTURES TRADES	41
LOW CAPITAL REQUIREMENT	42
BET DOWNWARDS WITHOUT MARGIN	42
MULTI-DIRECTIONAL PROFITS	43
PLAY BANKER	43

CHAPTER 6: BUILD A STRATEGY 44

ALWAYS HAVE A PLAN	44
NEVER SKIP ON RESEARCH	46
LEARN TO MANAGE YOUR EMOTIONS	48
ALWAYS KEEP AN EYE ON THE FEATURES OFFERED BY YOUR BROKER	49

CHAPTER 7: TECHNICAL ANALYSIS 52

PRICE CHARTS	54
CHART PATTERNS TO BE AWARE OF	56

CHAPTER 8: THE STOCK MARKET TREND 58

THE MARKET IS UPTREND	58
THE MARKET WITHOUT TREND	59
TREND LINES	60
CONDITIONS OF EFFECTIVENESS OF A TREND LINE	60
FINDING A TREND REVERSAL USING A TREND LINE	62
CANALS OR CHANNELS	63
INTERMEDIATE LINES	64
RUPTURE OF THE CANAL	65
PRECAUTIONS WHEN DETECTING A SIGNAL	65
HOW TO DETECT THE END OF A TREND?	66
THE TREND REVERSAL	66
HOW ARE TRENDS FORMED?	67

CHAPTER 9: THE RULES TO FOLLOW IN THE STOCK MARKET 68

HAVING KNOWLEDGE ABOUT THE TIME FOR IMPROVISING THE PLAN	68
AVOIDING TRADES THAT ARE OUT-OF-THE-MONEY	69
PREPARING THE ENTRY AND EXIT PLAN BEFORE STARTING	70

CHAPTER 10: HOW TO INVEST IN STOCKS, FOREX, SWING, AND DAY TRADING AND RELATED STRATEGIES 74

FOREX TRADING FOR BEGINNERS	74
ESSENTIAL STOCK SALES RULES	77
TRADING IN OPTIONS	82

CHAPTER 11: BASIC RULES SOFTWARE AND GUIDELINES FOR NAVIGATING THE TRADING PROCESS 84

CONCLUSION 90

Introduction

Options trading has been the focal point of much discussion of ongoing years. Is it risky? Would we be able to go bankrupt? For sure, options as a type of subsidiary instrument is unmistakably more perplexing than the stocks that they are composed dependent on and, similar to a wild stallion, can hurt you if you don't see how it functions and how to utilize it appropriately.

In this part, I will exhibit 5 reasons why options trading is, in reality, superior to anything stock trading to scatter the well-established legends of how perilous options trading is. We should recollect this: Options trading is hazardous just when you don't get it.

1) Variable Leverage

The influence that options give you is maybe the main motivation behind why individuals incline toward options trading in any case. In any case, in options trading, you could be making a 10% benefit on that equivalent 1% move the stock made or even up to 100% on that equivalent 1% move!

Indeed, the excellence of influence in options, not at all like in prospects trading, is that it is VARIABLE!

You could take on more impact for more peril, or lesser significance for lesser risk by picking choices of different strike costs and also end month. The more out of the cash choices, the higher the impact, and the more in the cash choices the lower the impact.

Influence cuts the two different ways. This is the reason the excellence of control in options trading is that it enables you to make similar trades with a lot lesser money, all things considered, you could primarily utilize just money you can bear to and plan to lose in any fizzled trade for every alternative, so influence helps you control your misfortunes!

2) Low Capital Requirement

Apple Inc., AAPL, is trading at $295.36 today, which implies it takes $29,536 to buy 100 offers today. In any case, AAPL's at the money call options costs just something like $715 to control the profits on that equivalent 100 offers of Apple!

3) Bet Downwards Without Margin

To benefit from a downwards proceed onward a stock in stock trading, you could short the stock which causes edge. In options trading, all you have to do to wager on a stock going downwards is to BUY its put options with no margin required by any means. It's hard to believe, but it's true, buying put options for the benefit to drawback works precisely equivalent to buying call options for the benefit to the upside. There is no compelling reason to possess the stock previously, and there is no requirement for the edge!

4) Multi-Directional Profits

In stock trading, you conceivably advantage when the stock goes toward the way you need it to. Upwards when you purchase the stock or downwards when you short the stock. There is no exact method to profit in the two circumstances simultaneously, and there is no down to earth approach to help if the expense of the stock doesn't move. In any case, in choices exchanging, such multi-directional benefits are possible! A few choices techniques empower you to profit, paying little mind to if the stock goes upwards or downwards quickly, and some choices systems benefit independent of whether the expense of the capital remains unaltered! Such is the untouched charm of choices philosophies which colossally manufactures your chances of winning in alternatives exchanging versus stock exchanging!

5) Play Banker

Weary of continually being at the player's side of the table? In options trading, you could change slightly to the investor's side of the table and do what market producers do by selling options to individuals who are needs to take the bottom of the player! At the point when the players lose, as they frequently do, you get the opportunity to keep the wager as a benefit only like a genuine investor! Just options trading has the "wager," which you had the opportunity to, and it is known as "outward esteem."

Understanding The Importance Of Options Trading

If you are into trading, you will most likely think about options trading. A great many people expect that they realize every one of the terms identified with trading options and proceed with their trading techniques. Web-based trading has made tremendous advancement, and you have to stay up to date with all the new happenings. You will likewise need to look at the forex options when you are doing web-based trading.

The criticalness of an option has numerous implications, and you need to understand this word well, indeed, without a doubt while doing the online exchanging. A decision is a cash related instrument that is gotten from the expense of the hidden apparatus.

Nuts and bolts Of Online Trading

A choice is of two sorts. The first kind is the call alternative, and the second is the put choice. Understanding the call and put options is very imperative to pick up mastery in web-based trading. When taking a gander at the trading options, you will likewise need to deal with your accounts appropriately and contribute carefully. It is additionally essential to know the various methods for how to trade options in the present market situation. If you need to make the most extreme bit of leeway of the unpredictability in the wares market, you should evaluate the FCD trading.

The key terms that you have to comprehend when you are doing web-based trading are Commodities Trading, Trading Commodities,

Trading Metals, Options CFDs, stock records, Stock Index CFDs, Index Trading, Stock Index Trading, CFD Trading, CFD Provider, and CFDs. The ideal approach to get some data on these terms is via seeking them on the Internet. When you are obtaining wholly befuddled, it bodes well to look at with somebody who knows these terms appropriately. You may need to go through at any rate seven days in understanding these terms.

When you are OK with these terms, you should get into the systems for trading. As of now, trading gold may appear to be generally amazing and painful. However, numerous different options would likewise give you a similarly decent return. In all stock market trading deals, it is seen that individuals do the buying and selling without really understanding the essential rules. If you are keen on CFD trading or contract for distinction trading, you should initially comprehend the rudiments of CFDs, the way toward trading CFDs, and distinguish the dangers that are included amid contract for contrast trading.

The contract for contrast trading is best comprehended when a model is taken. Along these lines, discover a site that will give you the precedents. After you have a website that offers all of you the best models, you should proceed onward and look at the procedure of agreement for distinction trading. When seeing the precedents, you might be blessed to receive a few numbers and figuring's.

Such computations are inescapable, and you need to hold up under with it. For the most part, with a little practice and great fundamentals, you will have a more precise comprehension of the methodology and ideas of the agreement for distinction trading. Choosing the best site for your options trading is significant. In this way, ensure you get a decent place for all your trading necessities.

Chapter 1 The World's Greatest Opportunity Machine

Why Use Options?

Why should you use options? Here are a few reasons why you should utilize options as your tool for trading.

- You only need minimum initial cash outlay to purchase options as compared when buying stock in trading.
- Options such as call options enable investors to enter the market at a cheaper cost.
- Options also help investors to generate more income. It is seen mostly by using the covered call options trading strategy. The investor holds on to the stock believing the price will have few changes. It is either to remain stable or increase a little.
- Purchasing calls and put options enable traders to invest with minimal risks since the primary thing they can lose is premium.
- Using options will offer you more investment alternatives since it is a flexible trading tool.

How Options Work

After knowing the strategies and the reasons why to use options, let us now know how this type of trading works. Below are some of the details I have for you:

- Options have a time frame. They always have their date of expiration. You should be able to know their time frame to make profits. After they expire, you do not have the right to purchase or offer stock for sale at a specified price. The shorter the time it has till expiry, the lower the value of the option.
- Options have different strike prices, which generally indicate the price of the stock.
- Options offer you the right to purchase or offer stock for sale.
- Purchasing an option gives you the honor to purchase or offer the stock for sale.
- Selling an option gives you the honor of delivering the stock at an agreed price. The stock's current price is not under consideration.

Cons of Options Trading

- It is a sophisticated type of trading.
- Options trading is very ambiguous. Traders need to observe the best and worst-case scenarios keenly to generate massive profits. It is time and energy consuming

- mostly for the less experienced traders who are not aware of the different strategies that you need to implement.
- Most traders also have no idea of the volatility of the prices in the market. Furthermore, it is tough to get information on options trading in magazines.
- Any gains made in this trading are all taxed. The tax rates are so high for the traders ending up getting less money from the trading.
- Options have an expiry date. Buyers participating in options trading should be aware of the expiry date. The value of an asset decreases with time to its date of expiry. Many traders fail to observe this ending up purchasing assets with less value.
- Options trading has high commissions for the amount invested. The commissions for this trading can also be higher for spreads.
- Risks involved in options trading are unlimited. You need to be alert all the time and observe market behavior.
- Options are available only to some market securities, unlike stock trading. It makes it tough for most traders.

How Much Capital Is Needed?

Do not rush to waste your cash. There are too many risks in this type of trading. Capital is a basic requirement to start any business. Does options trading require too much capital? No. When starting on options trading, it is better to start with small capital to avoid massive trading risks.

Many are the individuals who utilize much of their cash for trading during their first days, which is so dangerous. Such individuals end up having too many risks to handle, and finally, they make up their minds to close their businesses. I do not want you to fall into such a mess. Do your thing with the right speed.

Start options trading with a reasonable small amount. Do not brag off that you got everything under control. You will lose even the only cash you had. Starting with less money has a high likelihood of fewer risks in trading. I bet you can now handle a few risks and be able to continue with your trading.

Chapter 2 How to Get Started with Stock

Options trading has helped many investors to manage and grow their portfolio. Through the knowledge of options trading, many investors have protected their asset portfolio from risks and increase returns. The key is to know how to play the game and win.

Even though we have seen and heard the stories of many people how have become enormously successful in options trading, many people still have fears. You don't have to be afraid of trading in options because of the underlying risks. As with all investments, there is an amount of risk. To lower the risks, you have to know what you are doing. When you have better clarity about what you're doing, it limits your risks and set you on the path of success. By learning the basics of options trading and using the basic strategies to maximize your gains, you'll find yourself doing well in options trading. As a beginner options trading, what you have to do is to make sure you calm yourself down and start taking steps to begin your trade.

Options Trading Account

Your trading account is where all options trading activities will be done. Basically, an options trading account is a system or platform used by an investor to purchase and buy financial securities such as stocks, indexes and many others. The trading account is held by the brokerage firm and used to manage trading activities on your behalf. With an online trading account, you can hold cash, stocks, and another type of securities.

Technology has made it easy for managing trading accounts. To start using your trading account, you must first of all fund it. Many people think they can use a cheque from a friend to fund their options trading account. Well, that is not allowed. Your bank account will be connected to the trading account. Through bank wire or transfer, you can transfer funds into the brokerage account through your savings or checking accounts.

Another factor to consider is a tax. Your trading account can be taxable or tax-deferred like a 401 (k). You can also decide if your trading account will be a taxable or simply a nonretirement account. You can choose to open an individual account or brokerage account for your business to trade. These are just forming of trading account, but there are two main types based on their functionality: margin and cash trading account.

Margin vs. Cash Trading Account

Margin Trading Account: A margin account is simply a brokerage account that provides you with a line of credit to buy options, stocks, and other securities. Are you planning on using leverage for your trading? Through a margin trading account, you can borrow money to buy stocks or options. This gives you a form of leverage if you don't have cash at hand to purchase securities.

What you need to know about the margin trading account is that all margins come with an interest. Each money borrowed to you for trading has an interest associated with it. That means for each that trade you are successful with; the brokerage account has to deduct taxes, fees, and interests used in purchasing the securities.

The typical rate is 2% over the prime interest rate. An Intraday Margin Account, for instance, works on 4 to 1 leverage ratio. That means for every amount of equity that you have; you will be granted access to credit four (4) times that amount. Let's say that you have a cash amount of $ 1,000 through an intra-margin account you can borrow as much as $ 4,000 for your trading activities.

Cash Trading Account: A trading account deals with only cash. There is no line of credits for you to borrow the securities you deem feasible for you. All trading transactions in your account will be done via the cash you have transferred into the trading account via your savings or checking bank account. This account means you have no form of leverage for all trading decisions. For instance, when you placed $ 1,000 into your cash trading account, the only money available for you to spend in buying and trading securities will be that $ 1,000.00. If you don't close any position in your trading account, you will not have any line of credit to provide you with purchasing power. The settlement date for cash accounts varies, but they can be as short as the day of the transaction and the following one.

Steps to Open a Trading Account

1. Providing Personal Information

To open a trading account, the brokerage firm will require you to provide certain personal financial information. This financial information helps the broker to track, manage and handle your account. You need to be careful you provide the right details to facilitate smooth trading activities. The sign-up process for a brokerage account varies from one broker to another, but the personal information required to run the account is almost the same.

2. Providing Additional Information

The following is the information to be provided: Legal name, email address, social security number, employment status, approximate annual income, and others. Some brokers want to know your experience level in trading underlying securities like stocks, index funds, and options.

Are you a registered broker-dealer? Are you managing a brokerage account on behalf of an individual or an institution?

Are you a shareholder in a company assigned to manage the brokerage account for the company? All this additional information will be asked to enable the broker to tailor their services to you. A special disclosure obligation will also be provided to authenticate and protect the information provided.

3. Idle Cash Management

If you have idle cash in your brokerage account, how will it be managed? Your broker would want to know how you intend to handle or manage the account. For example, you have invested and earned $ 16,500 worth of money. You have decided to trade in other securities with $ 10,000, what would you like the idle 6,500 to do? You might want to instruct the broker to push it into interest-bearing accounts such as treasury funds, mutual funds, or even the money markets.

4. Trading Account Suitability

There are various kinds of trading styles. Your broker would want to know the best way you want to handle risk and manage trading activities. It is the goal of the broker to know the customer and provide the best support and services to be successful in trading activities. Some of the trading styles can be: aggressive growth (more risk-taking in volatile securities), Simple Growth (gain money while preserving original capital), Income Risk Level (using income generate from profits for further trading) and Conservative (capital preservation and using the account of only one thing to protect existing assets).

5. Signing Account Opening Agreement

Before the trading account is opened, the broker would ensure that you sign and approve all the information provided. You might want to review all the information provided as well as read the contract statement to know the terms, policies, and conditions used by the broker in managing the trading account. Once you are done, you can then confirm to agree with the terms for the trading contract. An electronic signature, print & sign or mail & sign will be used.

7 Easy Steps to Start Options Trading

To begin options trading, the following are some things to get started with:

1. Initial Preparation
2. Choosing an online broker
3. Finding your options trading niche
4. Finding option trades opportunities
5. Planning individual trades
6. Risk and money management
7. Monitoring your trades

Chapter 3 Day Trading Options That Actually Works

Call Options

A call option gives the investor the right (not the commitment) to buy the fundamental stock, security, item, or other instruments, at a particular cost within the time of the contract. The predefined cost is known as the strike cost. A speculator who is bullish on the stock, which means he anticipates that the stock should go up within a short time or inside the particular time span, would buy a call option.

For instance, say Investor A thinks stock XYZ is going to post high income one month from now, and the stock will go higher. So she buys a call option on the stock for $20. The option agreement determines that she can buy 100 portions of XYZ at a strike cost of $100 inside the following 60 days. If the cost of the stock falls beneath $100, then she won't practice the option. The agreement will terminate uselessly and she will have lost the $20 price tag. In any case, if the cost of the stock transcends $100, state to $130, then she will practice the option, buy the stock for $100, and afterward, sell it at the higher market cost. She has now made a pleasant benefit.

Put Options

A put option is something contrary to a call option. It gives the owner the right (however not the commitment) to sell the fundamental stock at a predetermined value (the strike cost) inside the predefined time span. An investor who is bearish on the stock, which means he thinks the stock cost is going down, would buy a put option.

For instance, say Investor B thinks stock XYZ is overrated and will decrease in cost throughout the following 60 days. He buys a put option on the stock for $20. The agreement gives him the option to sell the stock for $120 inside the following 60 days. If the stock transcends $120 per share, then he would not practice the option. It would lapse useless, and he has lost his underlying speculation. If rather the cost of the stock dips under $120, to state $90, then he would practice his entitlement to sell the offers at $120 and pocket the distinction as a profit.

Using Call and Put Options to Make a Profit

There are various ways you can use call and put options. For instance, assume you believe that portions of US banks that are as of now selling for $200 per share are undervalued and will go higher in the following couple of months. You need more money to buy at least 100 portions of stock, yet might, in any case, want to bring in money from the ascent in the stock. For this situation, you could buy a call option on the stock, which would cost just a small amount of the cost of the stock. So you buy the call option, and you presently reserve the option to buy 100 portions of the stock at $200 whenever in the following 60 days.

You may be thinking, how am I going to buy the stock in the next 60 days for $200 per share if I don't have the money? The appropriate response is that you don't really need to buy the stock to make a profit. If your impulses are right and the stock cost rises above $200, then your call option will turn out to be increasingly important. At the end of the day, as the stock value rises, the value of your option agreement likewise rises. You will have the option to sell the option agreement itself, rather than the stock, and make a benefit. The higher the value rises, the more your agreement will be worth.

This works a similar route for a put option, but in this situation, you need the stock cost to fall. As the cost of the hidden security drops, the value of your put option will rise. The further the value falls, the more important is your option.

As should be obvious, by buying options, you can make a profit whether or not the stock is going up or down in cost.

Styles of Options

The past segments have given a review of the two essential sorts of options, calls, and puts. This segment will assist you in understanding the different styles of options accessible.

Most options that you will buy will can be categorized as one of two classifications, American or European. These are once in a while known as vanilla options. The principle distinction between the two is the point at which you can practice the option.

American Options

American options can be practiced whenever before the expiry date. Most options on stocks and value are of this sort. These are additionally the kind of agreements exchanged on fates trades.

European Options

European options must be practiced on the lapse date characterized in the agreement. These sorts of options are, for the most part, exchanged over-the-counter (OTC) advertise.

The values of the two options styles are determined marginally distinctively, and their termination dates are additionally unique. American options lapse the third Saturday of the month, while European options terminate the Friday before the third Saturday of the month.

Similitudes between the two incorporate the result and the strike cost. The result, either for calls or puts, is determined similarly for the two kinds. In like manner, the strike costs ordinarily are the equivalent.

Extraordinary Options

While the over two styles are the primary ones most investors will manage, there is an assortment of increasingly colorful option sorts to know about too.

Bermuda Options

Bermuda options are in the middle of American and European options. In this kind of option, you are permitted to practice them on numerous dates during the agreement time frame.

Barrier Options

Barrier options are not the same as different sorts talked about so far in that all together for the option to result in the cost of the basic security must cross a specific level. They can be either be put or call options. There are four sorts of barrier options, which are plot beneath:

*Down-and-Out Barrier Options: A Down-and-Out Barrier Option gives the holder the privilege however not the commitment to buy (on account of a call) or sell (on account of a put) portions of a hidden resource at a foreordained strike cost since the cost of that advantage didn't go beneath a foreordained barrier during the option lifetime. That is, when the cost of the hidden resource falls underneath the barrier, the option is "took out" and no longer conveys any worth. Henceforth the name out for the count.

*Down-and-In Barrier Options: A down-and-in option is something contrary to a done for barrier option. Down-and-in options possibly convey value if the cost of the fundamental resource falls beneath the barrier during the options lifetime. If the barrier is crossed, the holder of the down-and-in option has the option to buy (if it is a call) or sell (if it is a put) portions of the hidden resource at the foreordained strike cost on the termination date.

*Up-and-Out Barrier Options: An up-and-out barrier option is like a done for barrier option, the main contrast being the arrangement of the barrier. Instead of being taken out by falling beneath the barrier cost, up-and-out options are taken out if the cost of the hidden resource transcends the foreordained barrier.

*Up-and-In Barrier Options: An up-and-in barrier option is like a down-and-in option; anyway, the barrier is set over the present cost of the hidden resource, and the option might be substantial if the cost of the basic resource arrives at the barrier before lapse.

Basket Options

A basket option, otherwise called a rainbow option, is an agreement wherein the worth depends on at least two basic resources. The option to practice the option is reliant on the costs of every fundamental resource.

Capped Style Options

In this kind of agreement, the most extreme benefit is set up. Capped options contain an arrangement where the option is practiced consequently if the fundamental security arrives at a specific set up cost. These kinds of options offer the author of the option a most extreme sum that can be lost.

Compound Options

These are fundamentally options to buy an option. Additionally called split-expense options on the grounds that the holder must compensation two premiums, one forthright and one if the option is worked out.

Lookback Options

This style of option supplies to the holder the option to either buy or sell the fundamental security at its top (on account of calls) or most reduced (on account of puts), cost over a predetermined time span.

Asian Options

Asian options, otherwise called normal options, are those where the result is dependent upon the mean (normal) cost of the fundamental security over a particular period of time.

Binary Options

Binary options have a payout that is either a fixed sum or nothing by any stretch of the imagination. There are two sorts: money or-nothing and resource or-nothing. In the primary kind, the holder would get a fixed measure of money if the option lapses in-the-money. In the advantage or-nothing assortment, the holder would get the value of the hidden security. Otherwise called digital options, win big or bust options, and fixed bring options back. The bit of leeway to this kind of option is that the potential return is a known sureness before the option is bought. Notwithstanding, once bought, they can't be sold before the lapse.

Forward Start Options

Forward beginning options start with a vague strike value that will be resolved later on.

LEAPS

LEAPS stands for Long-term Equity Anticipation Securities. LEAPS are basically equivalent to customary options with the exception of the more drawn out lapse dates. A LEAP can have a lapse date that is as long as three years away. The favorable position to this kind of option is there is much more opportunity for the basic stock, and along these lines option, to move toward the path you need it to.

Index Options

Notwithstanding buying options on singular protections, you can likewise buy options on a stock list. These can be engaging even though they give an introduction to a whole gathering of stocks. List options are adaptable and can fit into the systems of both moderate and theoretical investors, during both a bull and a bear showcase. Most file options are European style options.

Chapter 4 Secrets of The Stock Market

It would be useful in the event that we were given various lifetimes in which to idealize our techniques for exchanging and contributing. Shockingly, the total of what we have is this life and the present minute. What's more, that implies a great deal of trial and error.

However, trial and error don't imply that you should commit indistinguishable errors from every other person or, on the other hand, a similar number.

An expansive piece of the trial comprises of instructing yourself keeping in mind the end goal to eliminate the error partition. Also, the motivation behind teaching yourself, with regards to alternative exchanging, is to kill whatever number potential oversights as would be prudent in advance.

The three best option strategies for everyone

- Are there successful choice exchanging systems that don't require proficient review ability with a specialized investigation?
- Are there any moderately straightforward alternative techniques or strategies accessible to build one's profits without taking over the top dangers?

- On the off chance that these procedures exist and in the event that they're powerful, what makes them compelling?
- From a basic point of view, I can recognize three separate TYPES of option systems that can be exceptionally gainful for the ordinary trader. The one normal characteristic these techniques share is that at some level, in full or to some degree, they depend on offering time premium.
- Leveraged Investing
- Writing Covered Call Options for Income
- Calendar Spread Trading

What is Leveraged Investing?

More or less, this sort of options-based contributing endeavors to artificially impersonate fruitful esteem contributing - procuring quality assets as efficiently as could be expected under the circumstances and after that pressing a touch of something additional from those assets once you've obtained them.

Emphasis of the approach is always on the assets themselves, not the options.

In the event that it's not Quality Investing, at that point it's not Leveraged Investing. The options themselves are only instruments, in spite of the fact that they are intense devices that can give you immense edge over different financial specialists who are surrendered to paying the maximum for their stock and afterward waiting at the share cost to appreciate.

Experts of this style of contributing, be that as it may, look for not exclusively to gain their stock for a rebate however to keep bringing down their cost premise on the stock for whatever length of time that they possess it. Possibly, sufficiently given time and persistence, they could really bring down their cost premise the distance to zero (and past) and pay nothing for their stock (in fact, they paid for it with time itself.)

Despite the fact that this isn't get rich snappy, the quickened intensifying impacts will deliver long haul brings about fundamentally less time than customary long haul contributing.

Covered Call Writing

I get a kick out of the chance to consider covered call writing as basically leasing your stock however with a compulsory prerequisite that you give your inhabitants the chance to get you out in the event that they so pick.

Be that as it may, when you compose covered calls for money, you really need to be called out of the position.

Covered calls are preservationist in one perspective - the cost premise of your long stock is constantly decreased by the measure of the time premium you offer. That implies on the off chance that you compose at the cash or in the cash calls, the stock can really remain level or go down despite everything you make the most extreme benefit.

What's more, it likewise implies that regardless of the possibility that the trade does conflicts with you, despite everything you have a specific level of drawback assurance not accessible to the straightforward purchase and hold speculator.

Writing covered call options for money isn't about long haul contributing - it's tied in with gaining awesome here and now salary comes back with sensible hazard. On the off chance that you can normal 3% restores each month that likens to 36% a year (technically it's much more on the off chance that you factor in the intensifying impacts).

What is better, 3% (all things considered, and some of the time more) is feasible in case you're ready to explore some genuine entanglements related with covered calls:

- Enormous moves down in the share cost will blow through the trade's intrinsic constrained drawback security and can rapidly snowball into a considerable misfortune.
- Since the accentuation is on here and now salary instead of long haul increases, some fundamental abilities or instruments including specialized investigation are basic.
- Distinguishing the best covered call trades can be troublesome, if certainly feasible, all alone and progressively.

These are genuine dangers and concerns, yet fortunately they can be tended to and limited, making this a feasible pay technique.

Covered call options for money can be a compelling methodology in an assortment of business sectors - bull, bear, or range-bound. A gentle bull advertise is clearly the most straightforward condition for covered call writing, yet even bear markets can, in any case, be productive on the off chance that you make some fundamental changes (giving the market doesn't endure an entire emergency, for example, what happened in October 2008).

Calendar Spread Trading

The center rule of this approach continues as before - benefiting from the way that an option's opportunities esteem rots at a considerably higher rate on here and now options than it does on long haul options.

That is a moderately basic and direct articulation, however the suggestions are significant. In case you're new to calendar spreads, the trade may appear somewhat confused at first. Be that as it may, in the event that you can recollect the "spread" idea of the trade, it turns out to be substantially less difficult to get a handle on.

In actuality, you're purchasing a spread between an option's close term time esteem versus an option's long haul time esteem.

As lapse (for the fleeting option) nears and arrives, and all else being equivalent, the transient option will quickly lose time esteem. Subsequently, your spread - and in this manner your increases - will extend.

Chapter 5 Why Stocks Are Good Investments

When it comes to working with an investment, you want to make sure that you are working with a choice that will make you money. No one wants to get into an investment that will have them lose all their money. But part of the point of an investment is that it does carry some risk. Hopefully, you are able to pick out an investment that has a much higher reward than a risk to it so that you can earn money. There are a variety of options that you can choose when it comes to your choice in investments. You can choose to do real estate, to put the money in retirement, trade on the stock market, and even start your own business. With all of these other options to choose from, why would you want to choose options as your investment vehicle? Here are some of the benefits of choosing options trading over some of the other investment options when you are ready to put your money to work for you.

Limit Your Risk

A good reason to go with buying options is that you will be able to limit your risk down to just the amount of money that you pay for the premium. With other investment options, you could end up losing a lot of money, even money that you did not invest to begin with, but this does not happen when you are working with options.

Let's say that you saw that the prices of cows were about to go up. You could pay some money upfront and enter into a contract with someone else to sell your five cows for $ 2000. At this point, since you are working with an options contract, you did not buy the cows upfront.

On the other hand, if you had gone up to the other person and purchased those cows straight up for a cost of $ 10,000, you could end up in trouble. For this example, the price of the cows may end up falling by $ 500, rather than going up by $ 500, and you would end up losing $ 2500 in the process. Since you went into the options contract though, you would stand to lose no more than $ 250 if the prices were to fall afterwards. You still stand to lose some money, but it is a lot less than you would have lost otherwise.

Better Leverage for the Money

You will find that when you are working with options, it can provide you with some good leveraging power. A trader will be able to buy an option position that will imitate their stock position quite a bit, but it will end up saving them a lot of money in the process.

Let's say that you saw that there was an opportunity to make a profitable trade, you were only able to spare about $ 1000 to purchase the stock, but you didn't know that options were available. If we were still talking about the cows from before, you would not be able to purchase even one cow for the money (remember that they are about

$ 2000 each without the options contract), and so you would completely miss out on the possibility to make a profit.

But, if you decided to purchase with an options contract, rather than purchasing the underlying asset outright, the dynamics have completely changed. This could result in an investment of just $ 250 to get started. The premium on the options contract is a fraction of the total cost, allowing you to get in on the trade for a lot less money. If you look into options contracts, you will be able to make more purchases, and potentially more money, compared to some of the other stock choices you can make.

Higher Percentage of Returns

An options trader is only going to pay a fraction of the value of the asset just to have some control over that asset. This will allow the trader to earn more money than what they would be able to earn when they purchase the asset upfront and then try to sell it. Let's take a look at an example of how this can work.

Going back to the idea of the cows, the market price at the beginning of this trade is $ 2000. For a regular cattle trader, one who doesn't know anything about options, had the $ 2000 in hand, and believed that the price of the cattle is going to go up, he would only have the opportunity to purchase on cows. If the price of the cows goes up to $ 2500, this trader will only be able to make a profit of $ 500. This isn't bad, but since there is a big risk with this option, it is not always the best.

On the other hand, a trader who knows a bit about options will be able to do things a bit different. If you had $ 2000, you could choose to purchase eight options contracts, with a premium of $ 50. This means that you now have the purchasing rights for a total of 40 cows rather than the 1 cow the other trader had.

With the same profit of $ 500 per cow, your profit would be $ 18,000 (this includes the $ 500 per cow minus the $ 2000 you spent in the beginning to purchase the contracts). You earned thousands of dollars more compared to the original trader, but you used the same amount of money to get started.

Helps to Hedge Intraday or Futures Trades

It is common for traders to purchase or short-sell Futures contracts because they expect them to move in one direction or another. Intraday traders may do the same thing, because they will purchase a large number of shares in the hopes that they are going to move down or up during that day. If the trader ends up picking the wrong direction on the Futures or the intraday trades, they may end up losing a lot of weight. Unless you put in a stop-loss, it is possible for you to lose an unlimited amount of money in the process.

You may not be complaining when this goes the right way and you earn unlimited profits, but if you go with one of these trades and you don't hedge your position, you are going to complain when you start losing a lot of money. If you have an understanding of how trading options works, you could buy call or put options to help insure that you are not going to end up with an unlimited loss. The right options choice is going to help control your loss the moment that the intraday or futures positions start going against what you wanted.

While there are a lot of great investment choices that you can make, none of them are going to limit your risk as much as options while still providing you with a great potential to make money in the process. This is a great investment for anyone, whether they are just getting started with investing or they have been in the market for a long time.

Low Capital Requirement

Apple Inc., AAPL, is trading at $ 295.36 today, which implies it takes $ 29,536 to buy 100 offers today. In any case, AAPL's at the money call options costs just something like $ 715 to control the profits on that equivalent 100 offers of Apple!

Bet Downwards Without Margin

To benefit from a downwards proceed onward a stock in stock trading, you could short the stock which causes edge. In options trading, all you have to do to wager on a stock going downwards is to BUY its put options with no margin required by any means. It's hard to believe, but it's true, buying put options for the benefit to drawback works precisely equivalent to buying call options for the benefit to the upside. There is no compelling reason to possess the stock previously, and there is no requirement for the edge!

Multi-Directional Profits

In stock trading, you possibly benefit when the stock goes toward the path you need it to. Upwards when you buy the stock or downwards when you short the stock. There is no real way to benefit in the two situations at the same time, and there is no practical way to help if the cost of the stock does not move.

Play Banker

Weary of continually being at the player's side of the table? In options trading, you could change slightly to the investor's side of the table and do what market producers do by selling options to individuals who are needs to take the bottom of the player! At the point when the players lose, as they frequently do, you get the opportunity to keep the wager as a benefit only like a genuine investor! Just options trading has the "wager," which you had the opportunity to, and it is known as "outward esteem."

Chapter 6 Build A Strategy

Always Have a Plan

If you want to take options trading seriously, then it is extremely necessary to have a plan. This plan should have all the steps that you want to take and everything that you want to do. It would be even better if you write it all down. There are some beginners who go all in and they literally jump into the trade without knowing much about it. They have this attitude where they want to make as much money as they can but let me tell you something – this is an absolutely horrible strategy to follow. This is because the plan does not involve any strategy at all and you do not have any enter or exit plan in the trade. Basically, nothing is in place. If you are of the idea that you are going to wing it with options trading then trust me, you better give up now; otherwise, you are going to face huge losses.

So, when you make the plan, make sure that you have made it as detailed as possible. The first thing that you have to figure out is your expectation regarding how much profit you want to make through options trading. But this does not mean jotting down whatever figure comes to your mind. You have to be realistic about your expectations. In the first year of options trading, you are not going to make millions so quit having such high expectations. Another thing that you can do is make a note of all the things that are required when you decide to buy an option, and you should also note down what you want to see in each of those options.

Next, you can make a list of the strategies you want to implement. By now, you must have realized that there are tons of strategies that can be used, but what you will be using will depend on the type of situation you are in. The strategy also depends on the option you have chosen. Remember that it is not necessary for you to keep working with one single option throughout and if you change them in the right situation, then you can even have the chance of making more money, especially if you consider the long term. But do you know why I am asking you to write down the strategies? It is because of a very simple reason and that is – when you write down the strategies, they automatically become simpler and you can keep track of them in the same place. It will also help you make more money by choosing the right options.

Another thing to keep in mind is that you always need to have an exit strategy. And you need to figure it out before you even step into a trade. For starters, you need to think as to how much money you are actually willing to lose, or rather you can afford to lose. You also need to make a note of the conditions during which you will step out of the trade at all costs. Do you know what happens to those who do not have this information in place? They lose a lot of money simply because they do not know when to exit from a trade and they keep going even when it costs them everything. This happens mostly when someone is doing well and so giving up or leaving at the right time becomes quite difficult for them. This also happens when people stay in the trade because they are trying hard to gain back all the money that they have lost but this only makes them lose more money. So, when you have that exit strategy in place, you know what you have to do when things go south. So, having an exit strategy is truly one of the most important things in risk management.

So, now you might be feeling a bit overwhelmed because you think you have to figure out so many things before you can even start to trade. But what you need to understand is that you can take all the time you need, but you have to make sure that all this information is in place if you want to make profits from the trade. Making the right decisions will no longer seem that much tough and you will always have the path ready because you have planned it all before. You also know what your goals are so that you are not winging it. You are actually putting effort into the trade.

In case you feel confused with the process, and you are not sure whether your plan is good or not, you can consider talking with your broker. Since brokers talk with lots of people and they handle different kinds of traders, they can even help you out in framing the plan based on your requirements and expectations.

Never Skip on Research

Doing sufficient research before jumping into the world of options trading is very important. I have come across so many people in my who came into options trading just because they heard it from someone who made a big fortune, or they think that it is a very easy way of making money. There are so many people who think that they are going to get a big break overnight and they think that options trading is the best way to do so. It is true that with options trading, you can make some handsome amount of money but it is also true that you need to devote your time and effort and wait patiently before you get handsome results.

Doing your research thoroughly is very important, and you can call it a prerequisite of making a profit in the world of options trading. And if you are a beginner, it means that you have to do a lot of research because you start with nothing. But don't worry, once you start the research, everything will start falling into place. You need to learn different ways of studying the market and you also need to understand how to figure out the best time to invest in the market. Then, you also have to learn different strategies and know when to use what. But yes, in the beginning, you have to start by learning what options are and what is the difference between options and other forms of investments in the stock market.

There is basically no end to the amount of research you can do. So, take your time and learn it step by step. Don't rush into it and understand everything that you learn. Only then can you stay in the world of options trading in the long-term.

Learn to Manage Your Emotions

Whenever you let your emotions interfere with your trading strategies, you are bound to make mistakes, and things will go south. You might even end up losing all your money. Would you like that? No, right? Then, it is high time that you learn to manage your emotions effectively. Emotions have to be managed regardless of what plan you are following or what strategies you have in place. Even if you are doing well now does not mean that you will not become emotional tomorrow. So, learning to manage emotions is a basic lesson for options trading.

Emotions have the tendency to force people into making decisions that will work against them and make them lose money. It can be in any form. Sometimes people stay in the market more than it is necessary and sometimes, people leave too early and both these situations can make you lose money. Also, every successful trader has gone through a phase where they became emotional, but in the end, they learned to control themselves. So, even if you became emotional this one time, there is no need to beat yourself up for it. Learn from your mistakes and then grow from there. You cannot let your emotions control your decisions; otherwise making profits will become impossible.

If you have this basic nature of being too stubborn or emotional, then options trading is something that you should not consider right now. In this form of trading, you have to stick to the plan if you want things to work out in your favor. So, if you think you cannot do that and you might become impulsive then work on dealing with that first before you enter options trading. At times, options trading can get really emotional causing you to become overwhelmed, panicked, or even too happy from the profits you made. There are some people who are inherently good at managing their emotions and it comes naturally to them, but not everyone is like that. So, before you go in and risk all your savings, it is time to ask yourself what kind of person you really are and are you suitable to dive into options trading right now?

Always Keep an Eye on the Features Offered By Your Broker

Some people think that the broker is only the person who will perform some trades and help you with things you cannot understand, but there is a lot more to it than this. There will be times when you did not make the right call, but your broker might be able to help you out of the situation in some ways.

One of the ways in which brokers can help you is by providing an out-of-the-money rate. Options trading has a major drawback, that is, at times, people have the possibility of losing their entire money, but when your broker offers you out-of-the-money rates, then you will not go entirely broke and manage to get some of the money back. This is basically an agreement that the investor will make with the broker where the broker agrees to pay a certain amount of money invested back to the investor. It is true that you will still lose some money, but at least you will not lose it all.

But you also have to keep in mind that this feature is not provided by every broker in the market, so you have to keep an eye out on who is providing what. Don't settle for the first option you come across. There is another way in which brokers can help you and that is by giving the sell back feature. This is a feature that you can avail when you are about to incur a loss because you made a bad call. With the help of this feature, you will be able to exit before the options approach their expiration date. Of course, if you leave the trade early, up to 60% of your initial investment is lost, but it also means that you will not lose everything.

Chapter 7 Technical Analysis

When working with technical analysis you are always going to want to remember that it functions because of the belief that the way the price of a given trade has moved in the past is going to be an equally reliable metric for determining what it is likely to do again in the future. Regardless of which market you choose to focus on, you'll find that there is always more technical data available than you will ever be able to realistically parse without quite a significant amount of help. Luckily, you won't be sifting through the data all on your own, and you will have numerous technical tools including things such as charts, trends, and indicators to help you push your success rates to new heights.

While some of the methods you will be asked to apply might seem arcane at first, the fact of the matter is that all you are essentially doing is looking to determine future trends along with their relative strengths. This, in turn, is crucial to your long-term success and will make each of your trades more reliable practically every single time.

Understand core assumptions: Technical analysis is all about measuring the relative value of a particular trade or underlying asset by using available tools to find otherwise invisible patterns that, ideally, few other people have currently noticed. When it comes to using technical analysis properly, you are going to always need to assume three things are true. First and foremost, the market ultimately discounts everything; second, trends will always be an adequate predictor of price and third, history is bound to repeat itself when given enough time to do so.

Technical analysis believes that the current price of the underlying asset in question is the only metric that matters when it comes to looking into the current state of things outside of the market, specifically because everything else is already automatically factored in when the current price is set as it is. As such, to accurately use this type of analysis all you need to know is the current price of the potential trade in question as well as the greater economic climate as a whole.

Those who practice technical analysis are then able to interpret what the price is suggesting about market sentiment in order to make predictions about where the price of a given cryptocurrency is going to go in the future. This is possible due to the fact that pricing movements aren't random. Instead, they follow trends that appear in both the short and the long-term. Determining these trends in advance is key to using technical analysis successfully because all trends are likely to repeat themselves over time, thus the use of historical charts in order to determine likely trends in the future.

When it comes to technical analysis, the what, is always going to be more important than the why. That is, the fact that the price moved in a specific way is far more important to a technical analyst then why it made that particular movement. Supply and demand should always be consulted, but beyond that, there are likely too many variables to make it worthwhile to consider all of them as opposed to their results.

Price charts

Technical analysis is all about the price chart which is a chart with an x and y-axis. The price is measured along the vertical axis and the time is measured via the horizontal axis. There are numerous different types of price charts that different types of traders prefer, these include the point and figure chart, the Renko chart, the Kagi chart, the Heikin-Ashi chart, the bar chart, the candlestick chart, the line chart, and the tick chart. However, the ones you will need to concern yourself with at first are going to be included in any forex trading platform software and are the bar chart, the candlestick chart, the line chart, and the point and click chart which is why they are outlined in greater detail below.

Line chart: Of all the various types of charts, the line charts are the simplest because it only presents price information in the form of closing prices in a fixed time span. The lines that give it its name are created when the various closing price points are then connected with a line. When looking at a line chart it is important to keep in mind that they will not be able to provide an accurate visual representation of the range that individual points reached which means you won't be able to see either opening prices or those that were high or low prior to close. Regardless, the closing point is important to always consider which is why this chart is so commonly referred to by technical traders of all skill levels.

Bar chart: A bar chart takes the information that can be found in a line chart and expands upon it in a number of interesting ways. For starters, the chart is made using a number of vertical lines that provide information on various data points. The top and bottom of the line can then be thought of as the high and low of the trading timeframe respectively, while the closing price is also indicated with a dash on the right side of the bar. Furthermore, the point where the currency price opened is indicated via a dash and will show up on the left side of the bar in question.

Candlestick chart: A candlestick chart is similar to a bar chart, though the information it provides is much more detailed overall. Like a bar chart, it includes a line to indicate the range for the day, however, when you are looking at a candlestick chart you will notice a wide bar near the vertical line which indicates the degree of the difference the price saw throughout the day. If the price that the stock is trading at increases overall for the day, then the candlestick will often be clear while if the price has decreased then the candlestick is going to be read.

Point and figure chart: While seen less frequently than some of the other types of charts, a point and figure chart has been around for nearly a century and can still be useful in certain situations today. This chart can accurately reflect the way the price is going to move, though it won't indicate timing or volume. It can be thought of as a pure indicator of price with the excessive noise surrounding the market muted, ensuring nothing is skewed.

A point and figure chart is noticeable because it is made up of Xs and Os rather than lines and points. The Xs will indicate the points where positive trends occurred while the OS will indicate periods of downward movement. You will also notice numbers and letters listed along the bottom of the chart which corresponds to months as well as dates. This type of chart will also make it clear how much the price is going to have to move in order from an X to become an O or an O to become an X.

Trend or range: When it comes to using technical analysis successfully, you will want to determine early on if you are more interested in trading based on the trends you find or on the range. While they are both properties related to price, these two concepts are very different in practice which means you will want to choose one to emphasize over the other. If you decide to trade according to trend, then you are more interested in going with the flow and choosing stocks to trade while everyone else is having the same idea.

Chart Patterns to Be Aware Of

Flags and Pennants: Both flags and pennants show retracement, those are deviations that will be visible in the short term related the primary trend. Retracement results in no breakout occurring from either the resistance or support levels, but this won't matter as the security will also not be following the dominant trend. The lack of breakout means this trend will be relatively short term. The resistance and support lines of the pennant occur within a larger trend and converge so precisely that they practically form a point. A flag is essentially the same except that the resistance and support lines from the flag will be essentially parallel instead.

If you are looking for them, both flags and pennants are more likely to be found in the mid-section of the primary phase of the trend. They can last up to two weeks before being absorbed back into the primary trend line. They are typically associated with falling volume which means that if you notice a flag or a pennant and the volume is not falling then you are more likely actually seeing a reversal which is an actually changing trend instead of a simple retracement.

Head Above Shoulders Formation: If you are looking for indicators of how long any one particular trend is likely to continue, then looking for a grouping of three peaks in a price chart, known as the head above shoulders formation, can indicate a bearish pattern moving forward. The peaks to the left and to the right of the primary peak, also known as the shoulders, should be somewhat smaller than the head peak and also connect at a specific price. This price is known as the neckline and when it reaches the right shoulder the price will likely then plunge noticeably.

Chapter 8 The Stock Market Trend

The Market Is Uptrend

A bullish market is characterized by a succession of lower and higher points, and higher and higher points. In a clear uptrend, the corrective phases (drop legs) are less important in amplitude than the impulsive phases (legs of rising). This property is very important because it provides a valuable indication of the possibility of a trend reversal. When a corrective leg has a greater amplitude than the impulsive leg (bullish in a bull market), then the uptrend is likely to be challenged. The trader will have to reconsider the current trend and avoid positioning himself for the purchase under these conditions.

A downtrend market is characterized by lower and higher points, but also by lower and lower points. In this type of market, rebounds often have less amplitude than bearish legs, the main characteristic of a bear market. In a trending market, the movements that go in the direction of the dominant trend are still the most powerful. As for the uptrend, the turnaround can be anticipated. This requires the recovery to be larger than the last bearish wave.

The Market without Trend

In a trendless market, there is no clear trend, and low points and high points are often confused. Buyers and sellers are testing themselves and no clear consensus is at work.

According to Wilder, markets evolve in trend one-third of the time and do not draw any clear trend during the remaining two-thirds. This property is important because investors are often victims of momentum bias. They tend to mechanically prolong the recent course evolution. If the course progresses during the last sessions, they are convinced of the continuation of its rise, and many traders are trapped by positioning themselves around resistance or slightly above2. Conversely, in the case of a decline in stock prices, investors say that this decline will continue and are trapped by opening a position around major support.

The good trader can wait patiently for the right moment before opening a position. Professional traders seek to position themselves at the beginning of an impulsive movement and avoid exposure by taking unnecessary risks when the market is not predictable. Good traders are people who can adapt to changing market conditions. Markets fluctuate differently depending on whether we are in an uptrend, bearish trend or a trending market. In a bullish (bearish) market, the trader will be able to afford to buy (sell) up (down) and sell (buy) even higher (low), even if that is not ideal.

Trend Lines

Trend lines are often used by traders to identify bullish points in an uptrend and highs in a downtrend. In a bull market, the trend line goes through at least two low points. Conversely, in a downtrend market, the trend line will join at least two high points. It is possible to adjust trends over time based on new information: sharper, more marked trends may indeed appear as the trend initially traced becomes obsolete.

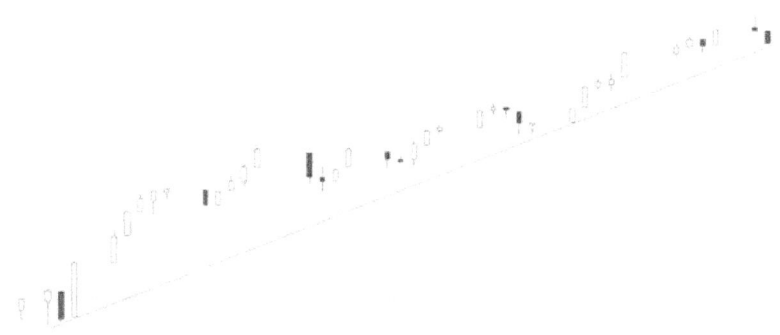

Conditions of Effectiveness of a Trend Line

The success of trend lines is justified by their effectiveness in identifying good levels of support and resistance. In other words, they sometimes make it possible to give with surprising precision these minor levels of reversal when a trend has already started. They also offer the possibility of identifying the state of the trend and anticipating reversals or simply corrective movements. In what follows, we try to give some elements to explain their effectiveness.

A first approach advances the argument of a stock market evolution respecting a "natural" phenomenon. There would exist on the market, and on all time horizons, trends that would respect a speed of progression and therefore a certain angle. The famous trader and analyst WD Gann explain that to last, a trend line must have a 45-degree angle. Not to mention natural phenomenon, we can say that a course of courses with a low slope indicates a slow movement that will probably abort. Conversely, when the slope is steep, the movement is too impulsive and will quickly run out of steam. The ideal is, therefore, to have an average slope (45 degrees), a sign of a healthy impulsive movement.

Another militant element in favor of trend lines is the fact that they are known to most operators. As we have seen, their validity will be strengthened because of the phenomenon of self-fulfilling prophecies. In concrete terms, a bullish trader will draw a trend line to identify the probable drop-off point for the stock, which will be a good buy with low risk. In the opposite case, it will draw a downtrend line to identify sales levels.

The importance of a trend line depends on the number of points it connects. The higher the number of rebounds on the right, the greater the importance. This is explained in particular by the mimicry of operators, which reinforces the strength of this line. Besides, the trend lines can be plotted over several time horizons (long, medium and short term), but the long-term trend lines or just to take them are those whose reliability is the most important. The trader will enjoy a return to the right of support (resistance) to strengthen its position buying (seller) and especially as the quality of the trend is proven.

Finding a Trend Reversal Using a Trend Line

The rupture of a trend line is an important reversal signal. This signal is all the stronger as the trend line is significant (it has been used on many occasions to support the current trend). The break of a bullish or bearish straight line materializes the end of a market dynamic: the operators who should have strengthened their positions near the trend line proved to be weaker than the opposing side (the bearers), thus allowing the rupture of the right and all the dynamics of the market. The change in trend thus seems clear.

A broken bullish straight line immediately becomes a line of resistance against which the market will crash; this is very often shown by a pullback (return to the right of a trend that has just been broken). The market is thus testing the strength of the support that has become resistant (or vice versa). Beware; the break of a trend line cannot alone constitute a signal of a reversal of the market, as shown by the example of the title PPR. It only alerts the trader about the possibility of consolidation.

Canals or Channels

A channel (Canal) is a figure directly related to the analysis of trend lines studied previously. The tracking is simple: once a bullish trend has been determined, it is a question of finding a parallel to the tendency to cover all the evolution of prices. Over the period when the trend is observed (straight line connecting the extreme points), we thus obtain a channel in which the courses evolve harmoniously.

The channel will tuck into a trend by allowing impulse turning points to be determined through trend lines, but also corrective turning points through the upper channel of the uptrend channel - or the bottom line for a downtrend channel.

The courses, thus vary between these two lines: the first constitutes the support line of the canal, where the courts come to rest; the second represents the resistance line of the channel (or top of the channel) against which the market stumbles.

As for trends, it is possible to distinguish short, medium, and long-term channels. The importance of a channel depends on its duration of evolution, but also on the number of times each line of the channel has been affected. To be considered a canal, you need at least two impacts on each side. The higher the number of impacts, the more important the channel is.

Intermediate Lines

In practice, prices do not move stubbornly between the lower bound and the upper bound. They sometimes have trouble passing intermediate areas within the canal. It is possible to draw parallel straight lines to the channel which constitute as many lines of support or minor resistance for the courses. However, the number of real intermediate rights is limited; one generally finds only one, even two. They are very often halfway through the channel and are real tests to know if the courses will reach the top or bottom. In the case of a bullish channel, the break in the intermediate resistance line often indicates that the market will reach the top of the channel.

It is also possible to distinguish within a channel small intermediate channels that allow, for example, the market to move from one terminal to another. Sometimes, too, a new channel emerges inside the canal, which appears more and more relevant, and which will eventually replace the old one that has become obsolete.

Rupture of the Canal

Two kinds of breaks can be envisaged: either the trend is confirmed and reinforced (it is an upward outflow of the uptrend channel or the decline of a downtrend channel), or it is reversed, and it is then a possible change of trend (downward release of a bullish channel and exit up a downtrend channel). The break is all the stronger as it is done in a large volume.

The operator has several elements to identify a possible rupture of the channel: in the case of a downward exit of a bullish channel, we usually notice that the courses have no strength, they do not arrive for example more to pass the intermediate right but stumble against it regularly. These elements are usually the first alarm signals.

Precautions When Detecting a Signal

The breaking of a bullish channel does not necessarily mean a sell signal, just as the break of a bearish channel does not always correspond to a buy signal. This is a simple indication that will need to be supported by other elements to become a relevant signal.

How to Detect the End of a Trend?

Can trend reversals be identified using chart analysis? We will see that it is possible to plot a reversal graphically, but for this, the trader will have to make sure that several criteria are respected: it is necessary to have a clear trend (for example, a trend line whose impulsive movements have a greater amplitude than corrective movements); the breaking of a major trend line or a major support is often a precursor signal of reversal; and finally, the various researches show that a figure of large turnaround (thus which took some time to be formed) will often be at the origin of an important corrective movement.

The Trend Reversal

After a downward movement (bullish), the title draws a bullish leg (bearish) whose amplitude is greater than the previous bearish (bullish) leg. This configuration signals a probable reversal of the trend and indicates the imminence of a bullish (bearish) departure or simply the cessation of the current trend and the entry of the market in a phase without a trend.

This presentation of trends has been deliberately simplified because the range of movements is much richer. Nevertheless, it is important to have a clear idea of the main trends in the markets before refining the analysis. The AGF stock is the typical case of a stock that draws a strong uptrend with very few corrections. It was difficult for a buyer to find a low point allowing him to position himself in the direction of the trend.

How Are Trends Formed?

Trends are a common phenomenon in the markets, but their training is often misunderstood by operators. Dow has developed a theory to provide relevant explanations for this phenomenon and can usefully be applied to current markets, regardless of the period used.

Chapter 9 The Rules to Follow In the Stock Market

In order to succeed in the world of options trading, you are required to trade by following certain rules and tips. All the tips that you will be found here can help you to achieve all that you wish to have in trading. Mistakes are meant to be made when you first start with trading. So, let's have a look at some of the basic rules of options trading and try your best to avoid mistakes.

Having Knowledge About the Time for Improvising the Plan

One of the most important aspects that are needed for successful trading is having a proper plan. But, besides that, you are also needed to take care of one more thing, and that is the perfect time for improvising your plans. There will be several instances when you will have to shift away from the plan. Your emotional aspects might also not work in such instances. To be successful in the world of options trading, you need to have proper knowledge regarding the time of the plan when it will be losing its validity. As you create a proper plan for trading, it can help you to set up a valid path for you. But, as you set up the path for yourself, that does not indicate you will be moved by the same path blindly right to the end of the world. Every trader needs to pass through a point of time in their trading career when everything seems to go out of hand. This will ultimately be making the proper plan to turn into something completely useless for that specific situation.

That is why, when you are having the thoughts of designing a new plan, you need to identify all its weak points. As you are the one who is creating all trading plans, you will have the proper knowledge when it can actually fail. The conditions of the trading market will keep on changing. So, what you have planned might work today but will not be the same the other day. If you are trying to keep on following your plan of action that has been predetermined even if the market condition gets turned 360-degree, you will be making a big mistake. When you keep on following a fixed plan of action, you are most likely to fail. You will surely need a lot of practice to understand the market scenario. The conditions will keep on changing. But, as you take a small step in the right direction, you can call it to progress. This also consists of being aware of the major differences that come between the present situation and the situation tomorrow.

Avoiding Trades That Are Out-of-the-Money

With the help of certain strategies, you can surely generate some amount of profit by purchasing out-of-the-money call options. But, such trades are only a few in numbers and can be treated as exceptions. As you enter the options trading world, you are most likely to get attracted like a magnet to the call options of out-of-the-money. In fact, it is very natural. The main reason behind this is that such options are affordable and cheaper than the others. But, you are also required to keep one thing in mind: the stock market and options market are different from one another. Even when you dedicate all your attention to the underlying security while buying options, that cannot be taken as a good strategy. It won't be a great idea if you are willing to purchase low and then sell them out as high. As a call option tends to be out-of-the-money, the chances of the same rising up again to the required levels before the expiry date are very low. So, if you are willing to purchase options of this nature, you will be doing nothing but gamble with all that you have.

Preparing the Entry and Exit Plan Before Starting

Trading of options is all about finding out the perfect positions of entry and exit. You are required to learn this thing first in the proper way before you start trading. No matter what kind of techniques you will be using for the adjustment, nothing can actually rectify a bad entry point. This might even result in you incurring a huge loss. But, there is something more important in options trading than fixing the proper entry and exit points. Do you have any idea what exactly it is? It is the knowledge of the fact that you need to exercise the entry and exit points much before you have given in all your capital.

Most of the beginner options traders have the notion that every trade they are going to make will bring them huge amounts of profits. They give their all for making the best out of the last cent spent by them. But, if you really want to succeed as a trader in the world of options, you cannot start following this idea. When you just aim to bring in huge amounts of profits, it can bring in new obstacles to your path. Until and unless you have a proper plan related to trading that can bring in profits as well, you will be performing a number of trades that can develop small profits. So, when you fix up your mind to stick to only one specific trade as if it is the only one left, you will actually be doing wrong. It will be resulting in huge losses for you.

So, once you have gained a potential amount of small profits from various trades, there is no need to think about the same again. You are only required to protect all that you have made. Of course, you can ignore this suggestion and keep on trading with your own trading plans. It can bring you more potential profits as well. But, the fact is that the loss you will be incurring will be much more than the actual profit. You might lose all your profit without even getting the chance to use it properly.

Not Trading for Wealth

If you think of options trading in a way that the returns you will be getting will be more than 150% or so, it will be better for you if you just step back and try to reconsider your position. Certain investments can indeed bring in huge amounts of profits. But, all the trades that you are going to make will not be the same. Various options traders think that options trading will be making them rich in one night. But, in reality, nothing happens like that.

In case you have opted for options trading to generate wealth, you have made up a wrong notion about the trading of options. Options trading is all about working with the perfect strategy to make sure of a daily income flow. As you try to be hungry for grabbing huge profits, there are chances that you will be overseeing the risky aspects. Never forget that options trading is very risky in nature. If you take one wrong step, all that you have can vanish in a second.

Chapter 10 How To Invest In Stocks, Forex, Swing, And Day Trading And Related Strategies

Forex Trading for Beginners

A lot of individuals today need to wander into the Forex trading business to earn some fast returns. Anyway, everybody who expects to take up this trade must realize that it is fundamental for them to know the subtleties of the business preceding taking a plunge in it.

Forex for apprentices may not be as easy as it might appear to be, however, whenever traded with the correct trading strategies, there is no reason why achievement can't be accomplished. Amateurs Forex includes gaining the essential gadgets of the trade altogether and, after that doing the business in a progressively trained way.

In this day and age, one in each five-person needs to put resources into Forex and profit right away. This has made Forex trading world's most significant trade as far as exchange volume. Up to an individual can risk and have abundance to contribute Forex trading can be a profitable business.

Web-based trading has made things stunningly better whereby an individual can trade Forex from the solace of their homes, maintaining a strategic distance from the issues voyaging. This has likewise made Forex for tenderfoots too easy to even think about venturing into as they can get everything dealt with on the web. To make progress with apprentices, Forex, one should play the diversion particularly well.

Legitimate preparation and practice, however, can make novices trade like veterans and reap high returns.

It is a must for each apprentice in the Forex trade to be dedicated and wary while executing the trade options.

Forex for tenderfoots turns into an easy undertaking with a Forex broker. The Forex brokers empower novices to work with a demo account, which can be acquired for nothing.

It is seen that fledgeling Forex customers are tricked in by the Forex brokers by offering a free demo account, giving them a superior comprehension of the business, and would likewise provide the customers with a chance to contribute virtual money instead of real and avoid any risk.

This, in the end, causes the customers to pick up a lot of trust in the trade and leave them urged enough to join with the broker to contribute hard money.

There are various presumed Forex instructional exercises nowadays, which can give a lot of expertise to apprentices Forex applicants needing to put resources into Forex. If not all, at any rate, the rudiments of the Forex trading business, which is, however, the learning, an apprentice Forex competitor need to know, can be accomplished through a decent Forex instructional exercise.

After an apprentice effectively finishes the instructional exercise classes, they can apply the essential trading tips that they have learned in the instructional exercises in the underlying period of their trade execution.

Receiving a decent Forex trading methodology is one of the essential activities with regards to Forex for amateurs. This won't just come convenient in limiting misfortunes yet also in defeating them also.

Taking the assistance of a real risk/compensate proportion is another important fledgeling Forex tip. This demonstrates the sum planned to be made in the trade must be set preceding trade execution and must be equivalent or more than the quantity a trader can stand to lose.

Followers of this tip can doubtlessly discover Forex for novices intriguing in a higher number of ways than one.

Fruitful Forex trading accompanies tolerance, determination, promptness, and diligent work. A taught methodology towards benefit making can assist an individual with novice Forex in a long way.

Forex for tenderfoots can be intense from numerous points of view, yet it is a dream followed by millions. Forex instructional exercises and Forex trading aides can assist numerous with turning such dreams into reality and subsequently turned out to be huge players in the trade.

Essential Stock Sales Rules

Options are a form of financial derivative, and all that means is that it derives its value from an underlying security

Commodities and Futures (ETF):

The provenance of financial Options is in the trading of Commodity and Future contracts as these were agreements between two parties, typically farmers and traders looking for a future price for their next harvest crops.

The futures markets developed to help traders hedge and speculate on commodities, especially in the agricultural market. The options market, in turn, evolved from the futures market, hence, the similarities and the shared concepts. But, because commodities and futures deal with a physical asset, there are slight differences as to how they work. The seller of a commodity or futures option is still obligated to buy or sell the stock. However, exercising the contract is different as commodities and futures contracts set the price for delivery of a specific quantity of a physical item – a bushel of wheat, for example - to be delivered to a particular location on an agreed date. There is nothing similar in stock options as there is no need for physical delivery of anything. Commodity options are options listed on such things as corn, oil, gold, or interest rates. Futures, on the other hand, are options trading on the underlying value of futures contracts, typical futures on commodities and currencies. Futures contracts are, therefore, derivative contracts –

their value is derived from the underlying commodity/asset - that give holders the obligation to buy or sell an asset at a specified future date for a specified price. Where there is a similarity between stock options and commodities and futures contracts is that they lock in the price and quantity of an asset and have predetermined expiration dates. But in both cases, they are in themselves tradable assets, which means you can trade away your rights and obligations if you wish to exit the contract early.

Equity Options

An equity option is an option based on the price of a share of stock of a company. However, options are not available on all stocks, but some do not have options attached to them. It is up to the exchanges to determine whether or not to offer an option – based upon perceived demand – it is not up to the companies that issue the stock.

Most equity options are priced at one contract per 100 shares. Equity options are what most people think of when they contemplate Options.

Index Options

The concept behind trading options in indexes is that if you can buy an option on a stock of a particular company within a sector says the technology, then why does the exchange not make available an option on that market sector as a whole?

That's the idea behind index options; you can bet on the sector performance and not have to drill down to a specific company.

The result has been a proliferation of Index options based on the performance of different market indexes. There are options on the S&P 500, NASDAQ, and FTSE. Trading in indexes has become a very popular alternative to trading in stock options as they can represent a collection of diverse assets.

This means that a trader can spread their investments across several sectors of interest. The index works by pooling together several stocks in the same sector or across diverse sectors, and the performance aggregate is used to measure the price of the group. There are many indexes, and these include stocks, commodities, and futures, as they are all used as components of an index.

But an index is just a logical category, a convenient grouping of other securities so you can't buy an index directly. Instead, you buy a security that tracks the value of the index. An example of such an option would be one that tracked a particular ETF that owned the stocks in a particular index such as Standard & Poor's (S&P) 500 Index.

Exchange-Traded Funds (ETFs)

ETFs are mutual funds that have become very popular trading vehicles as they can be traded like stocks on an exchange. Most ETFs are designed to track an index or an underlying sector, so technically, ETFs are not derivatives. However, they are often referred to as quasi-derivatives. This is because, unlike other indexes, they can be traded and also because they are not necessarily holding exactly the same securities of the index that they are tracking. For example, some leveraged ETFs use swaps to mimic the action of the underlying index while adding leverage.

ETFs allow you to trade on their underlying indexes, directly or through options. One of the most popular and well known ETFs is the S&P 500 SPDR (SPY).

Stocks and Bonds

Buying a company's stock gives you part ownership in that company, whereas buying bonds makes you a debt holder. Each position has its risks and rewards. However, when we bring Options into the equation, we can see that the three assets, stocks, bonds, and options, have very different risk and reward profiles.

In the end, stocks offer indefinite holding periods, and bonds have a maturity date, whereas options have a limited life based on their expiration date.

Interest Rate Options

These are sometimes better known as yield-based options, as they trade on the interest rate on a specific type of bond. With this type of Option, calls (buying) become more valuable as interest rates rise, and interest rate puts (selling) become more valuable as the rates fall. Importantly, the underlying value is the interest rate and not the value of the bond itself.

Because interest rates aren't securities and can't be traded or exchanged as such, the settlement is in cash.

Miscellaneous Options

The way that the different options exchanges make money and compete with one another is when they develop new innovative types of contracts that capture the imagination of hedgers and speculators. As an option is just a contract, which is based on the price of another asset, options can be drawn up for just about anything where someone might want to guarantee a price, and someone else might want to speculate on that price. As a result, exchanges are always trying out new option types, so you can find options on different measures of market sentiment, i.e., whether it's optimistic or pessimistic about different economic outcomes.

A Swap

This is a type of insurance contract whose terms are privately agreed upon by the participants. It is an over-the-counter style option as they are non-exchange traded options.

They are often used to bet on the direction of just about anything, including the weather, that the two parties agree upon. Swaps are by sophisticated design securities, and so they are not available to individual investors. This is due to the lack of regulations and the often complex financial and legal requirements required to be signed before you can trade them.

Trading in Options

As opposed to investing in stock or assets, to trade Options is often a decision based upon a short term analysis. An Option having a predetermined time period, a time-to-live, will have by design an expiry date. As a result, Options are renewable and can be resold many times. This makes them suitable for both tradings over the short term or over longer periods delivering income when the value of the underlying stock rises, falls, or even moves sideways.

Chapter 11 Basic Rules Software And Guidelines For Navigating The Trading Process

First, there are generally two sites which are seen as the "best" for options trading: OptionsXpress and TradeStation. Both of these have their own perks and their own reasons that you may decide to work through them.

OptionsXpress is a great place to start because they don't have an account minimum. They do ask a $12.95 commission on trades, and OptionsXpress only takes $1.25 for each contract. The fees can be a tad iffy depending upon your trade volume, but generally, the fees are low compared to other options. The other great thing about options trading by way of optionsXpress is that they have a lot of features that you'd really come expecting. For example, they offer real-time quotes and also allow you to look at options chains. Even better, optionsXpress doesn't charge you extra at all for using these tools. Bear in mind that in the world of finance, platforms will always favor those who are able to move more shares and who trade more often. But with that said, as far as a cost-effective options trading platform, OptionsXpress has you covered.

If you have a bit of money to invest, then you can go with TradeStation. TradeStation is generally ranked up there with optionsXpress in terms of really strong options trading platforms. And indeed, it's hard to find one much better than TradeStation. In exchange for a bit of a hefty account minimum, TradeStation offers you a huge amount of useful tools tucked right into their super handy platform. For example, you'll find yourself using features like automatic trade execution rather often. TradeStation is also built for people who understand technology such that they can develop, test, and sell their own trading strategies to other enterprising investors who may have an interest in such a thing. Of course, this doesn't mean necessarily that you have to use this utility, but it can certainly help you should you decide to use it. It has a high price tag with it, but it's very difficult to find a platform that is much better than TradeStation at what it's supposed to do: be a simple and straightforward platform which is highly extensible and super easy to build upon, should that be what you're wanting.

However, these can get rather convoluted. What if you just wanted simple, low-cost, and easy to understand, then it's hard to beat eOption. eOption is fantastic for low-capital investors who want the platform to just simply get out of their way and let them do their own thing. Options have an account minimum of $500, which isn't too much in terms of options trading, and their rates are extremely flat. They take a $3 trade commission, as well as fifteen cents for every contract that you decide to be involved with. If you haven't traded two times in the last year, or if you have less than ten thousand dollars in either your credit balances or your debit balances, you'll pay a fifty dollar fee for "account inactivity". They have an incredibly low margin rate, which means that their trading costs are low. The only place that you might get caught up is that they have a lot of data fees and platform fees. These can be a veritable cash rainbow of prices, and clock in at anywhere from $1 to $200 in a month, or possibly, even more, depending upon what all you're doing on the platform. As far as design and ease of use, there's not too much that's different from the others; there is an array of features that are available to you. Nothing particularly stand-out or amazing, but it certainly isn't a drab platform either. It's well-featured, and if you just want a simple and low-cost platform other than optionsXpress, it's incredibly difficult to find something that will fill those shoes better than Options.

In terms of powerful trading platforms, there are two reigning kings: TD Ameritrade and OptionsHouse. Both have their own perks. Either one of these has one of the highest tech and fully loaded trading platforms that you can ask for, as well as with specifically useful features that you as the end-user will find especially neat and handy.

TD Ameritrade doesn't have an account minimum and it takes a $9.99 trade commission. In addition, they have a promotion running which gives you six hundred dollars when you make a certain deposit. That can certainly be alluring in its own and give you a bit of extra capital to work with. TD Ameritrade operates on one of the most revered trading platforms in the business. Known as Thinkorswim, this platform is specifically created for active investors who are wanting the opportunity to get their hands on high-quality tools and research, as well as who would like to try out different strategies or practice cost observation by analyzing the risks and benefits of certain interactions they could make on the marketplace. In addition, TD Ameritrade offers the Trade Architect service, based on the internet, as well as a Mobile Trader application for smartphones and other mobile devices. Should one use Trade Architect instead of Thinkorswim, they'll find it lacking a bit in tools and services compared to the awe-inspiring Thinkorswim, but nevertheless they'll still find an absolute wealth of complex features that they'll find useful regardless.

The other super impressive platform that one may be interested in is aligned with the OptionsHouse eTrade broker. They offer a huge array of tools which are usually relegated to financial professionals who make an absolute career out of carefully watching and analyzing the markets in different ways. In other words, they have a huge number of tools that will benefit the type who wants to be an active trader. OptionsHouse too has a decent trade commission: $4.95 per trade. They don't have a specific account minimum, and they offer a thousand dollars in free commissions when you make a certain deposit.

Lastly, there are a couple of platforms that offer a great amount of utility in another way: the absolute wealth of market research and market data that they'll have available for free to any enterprising users who decide to use these services. In this category are Charles Schwab and Fidelity.

Fidelity has a $7.95 trade commission and a $2,500 account minimum. However, in return for this hefty minimum and hefty commission rate, you get access to one of the best stores of knowledge in the industry.

They get a huge amount of research, bigger than almost anybody else, and they offer a lot of research from over twenty industry giants, such as McLean Capital Management. They make it super easy to access all of this and it also comes free with your account. They also offer an application for your mobile device, which lets you access all of the research by way of your phone's built-in web browser. If you're looking for raw research, it's hard to do any better than using Fidelity Investments as your broker.

However, there is a tad more to knowledge than simply research, and Charles Schwab excels where Fidelity falls short. They have a $6.95 trade commission and a $1,000 account minimum. Additionally, they'll give you five hundred dollars in cash if you make a certain deposit, which once again could be useful for building up some expendable capital to use for your trading. In addition to a lot of raw research, Schwab has a tremendous amount of support for active traders, offering things such as trade assessment tools to allow you to see whether or not a trade you'd like to make is a bright idea. However, they also offer you a ton of options market discourse by the analysts hired by Schwab, as well as seminars, both live and pre-recorded, both online and in-person. What's more is that the in-person seminars are free to users of the service, because Schwab has a lot of branches throughout the country. What's more is that Schwab offers two top-notch platforms for stock trading. One is geared towards newer options traders, called StreetSmart, and the other is geared towards far more active traders, called StreetSmart Edge.

Really, knowing what options broker to go with is a matter of knowing yourself and your situation. Do you have a lot to spend on options trading? If you don't have a lot of investment capital, it's much better to start small and not invest too much in the first place, since your capital matters more to you by virtue of there being less of it. If you have a lot of investment capital and a basic idea of how to trade options, you'd be served well to go with one of the more research-heavy brokers geared at active traders. That too is a consideration in and of itself; do you want trading to be a significant part of your life? For example, do you want to do more with trading than just check the market every morning before work and night before bed? Do you want to spend a significant amount of time working on your portfolio and evaluating specific decisions to see which one would result in you making the biggest profit? If so, then you might find that you'd find yourself happier in the ones with a greater wealth of tools.

Conclusion

Trading Option can be extremely profitable but learning to trade them well takes time. You can choose to use indicators to determine your entry points, and I'm all for this approach at first, but remember that over the long term, you're better served learning the basics of order flow and using that.

There is no shortage of options strategies you can use to dramatically limit your risk and depending on the volatility levels, you can deploy separate strategies to achieve the same ends. Contrast this with a directional trading strategy where you have just one method of entry, which is to either go short or go long, and only one way of managing risk, which is to use a stop loss.

Spread or market neutral trading puts you in the position of not having to care about what the market does. In addition, it brings another dimension of the market into focus, which is volatility. Volatility is the greatest thing for your gains and options allow you to take full advantage of this, no matter what the Volatility situation currently is.

Options can be a bit hard to get your head around at first since so many of us are used to looking at the market as a thing that goes up or down. Options bring a sideways and a different vertical element to it via spreads and volatility estimates. More advanced options strategies take full advantage of volatility and are more math-focused, so if this interests you, you should go for them.

You can choose to borrow, of course, but you need to do this only if it is in line with your risk management math. Risk management is what will make break your results and at the center of quantitative risk management is your risk per trade. Keep this consistent and line up your success rate and reward to risk ratios, and you'll make money as a mathematical certainty.

Qualitative risk management requires you to adopt the right mindset with regards to trading, and it is crucial for you to adopt this as quickly as possible. Remember that the implications of your risk math mean that you need not be concerned with the outcome of a single trade. Instead, seek to maximize your gains over the long term.

The learning curve might get steep at times, but given the rewards on offer, this is a small price to pay. Keep hammering away at your skills, and soon you'll find yourself trading options profitably, and everything will be worth it. How much can you expect to make trading options?

I'm not keen on putting numbers to this sort of thing. Generally, good options trade can expect around 50-80% returns on their capital. As you grow in size, this return amount will decrease naturally. However, to start off with these are beyond excellent returns.

Always make sure you're well-capitalized since this is the downfall of many traders. You need to be patient with the process. A lot of people rush headfirst into the market without adequate capitalization or learning and soon find that the markets are far tougher than they thought. So always ensure the mental stress you place yourself in is low and that you're never in a position where you 'have' to make money trading.

The key to success is to simply never give up and to be resilient. Reduce the stress on yourself, and you'll be fine. Here's wishing you all the success in your options trading journey!

www.ingramcontent.com/pod-product-compliance
Lightning Source LLC
Chambersburg PA
CBHW051537240526
45465CB00027B/600